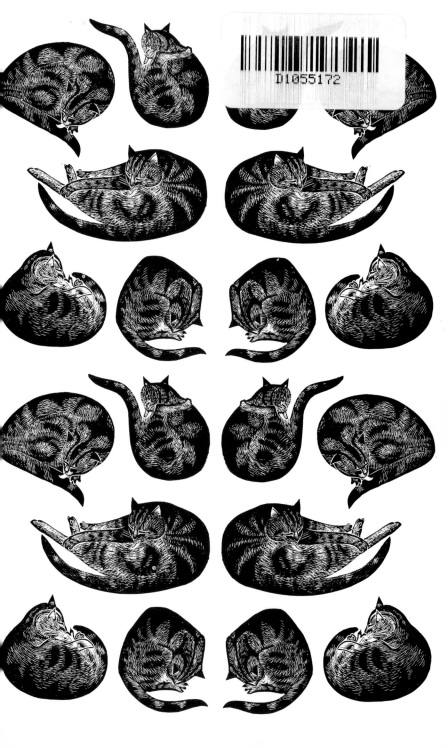

THE
IMPORTANCE OF
BEING
OSCAR

Yvonne Skargon

THE
IMPORTANCE OF
BEING
OSCAR

Wood engravings by Yvonne Skargon
Words by Oscar Wilde

SILENT BOOKS

First Published in Great Britain 1988
by Silent Books, Swavesey, Cambridge CB4 5RA

© Engravings copyright Yvonne Skargon 1988
© This edition copyright Silent Books 1988

ISBN 1 85183 004 9

Typeset by Goodfellow & Egan
Printed in Great Britain by
St Edmundsbury Press, Bury St Edmunds, Suffolk

I am OSCAR. Not Wilde, and far from wild.
Which is why, perhaps, we seem to have
some thoughts in common.

There is something tragic about the enormous number . . . who start life with perfect profiles, and end by adopting some useful profession.
Phrases & Philosophies for the use of the Young

*In nearly every joy, as certainly in
every pleasure, cruelty has its place.*
The Picture of Dorian Gray

*I couldn't help it. I can resist
everything except temptation.*
Lady Windermere's Fan

Industry is the root of all ugliness.
Phrases & Philosophies for the use of the Young

Anybody can be good in the country.
The Picture of Dorian Gray

*One's real life is so often the life that
one does not lead.*
Introduction to *Rose-leaf and Apple-leaf*

*To look wise is quite as good
as understanding a thing,
and very much easier.*
The Picture of Dorian Gray

One should always be a little improbable.
Phrases & Philosophies for the use of the Young

Those who find beautiful meaning in beautiful things are the cultivated.
The Picture of Dorian Gray

*The sure way of knowing nothing
about life is to try to make
oneself useful.*
The Critic as Artist

*Action . . . becomes simply the refuge
of people who have nothing whatsoever
to do . . . It is the last resource of those
who know not how to dream.*
The Critic as Artist

There is only one thing in the world worse than being talked about, and that is not being talked about.

The Picture of Dorian Gray

All charming people are spoiled.
It is the secret of their attraction.
The Picture of Dorian Gray

The first duty in life is to be as artificial as possible. What the second duty is, no one has yet discovered.
Phrases & Philosophies for the use of the Young

*To love oneself is the beginning
of a life long romance.*
Phrases & Philosophies for the use of the Young

There is much to be said in favour of modern journalism. By giving us the opinions of the uneducated, it keeps us in touch with the ignorance of the community.

The Critic as Artist

*None of us are perfect. I myself am
particularly susceptible to draughts.*
The Importance of Being Earnest

*Life is a dream that prevents
one from sleeping.*
From A Notebook

Oh, he is better than good —
he is beautiful.
The Picture of Dorian Gray

OSCAR *I wish I had said that.*
WHISTLER You will Oscar, you will.

AFTERWORD

Oscar Fingal O'Flahertie Wills Wilde was born in Dublin on October 10th 1854 and died on 30th November 1900 in Paris.

Oscar cat was born in obscure circumstances in north London in 1973. At the age of three months he adopted, courtesy the RSPCA, the wood engraver Yvonne Skargon and began an association with books and literature which has been acknowledged in works as various as Professor Samuel Schoenbaum's *Shakespeare, a Documentary Life* (Oxford University Press 1974) and Celia Hadden's *Gifts from your Garden* (Michael Joseph 1985). He has now retired to Suffolk where, when not posing for the pleasure of his many friends, he demonstrates Wilde's perception that 'in the country people get up early because they have so much to do, and go to bed early because they have so little to think about'.

The introduction of Oscar to Oscar was made by Jaqueline Watson to whom this opuscule is gratefully dedicated.